# THE ENGLISH RIVIERA

A s the sun sparkles on the blue-green waters of Tor Bay, setting the red sandstone cliffs aglow, it is easy to imagine the warm coral sea that occupied this stretch of English coastline millennia ago. Hope's Nose to the north and Berry Head to the south, remnants of a great barrier reef, mark the limits of the bay and mount guard over nearly 22 miles of award-winning beaches and secluded coves. Here are magnificent coastal walks, long stretches of sand, and rock pools and caves to explore. Beneath the waves, fish and other marine life abound, attracted by the many rocky outcrops, some of which contain traces of a former forest.

In this splendid setting stand the towns of Torquay, Paignton and Brixham. Torquay has grown from a small hamlet to a flourishing south-coast resort, host to international conferences and sailing events, while Brixham has largely retained its maritime traditions and still supports a busy fishing industry. Midway between the two is Paignton, formerly a small agricultural community but now a thriving holiday centre, with fine sandy beaches and entertainment for all the family.

The three towns owe their success largely to the gentle climate. The mild winters soon give way to spring and the gardens come alive with colour. The sheltered waters, which once provided safe anchorage for the Channel fleet, now offer a haven for water-sports enthusiasts of all descriptions – yachtsmen, anglers, wind-surfers, divers – who mingle amicably with the local boatmen. As a result the atmosphere has a distinctly Mediterranean flavour and, in the evening especially, as the lights begin to twinkle along the waterfront and the sound of the chugging ferry-boats drifts gently shorewards, Tor Bay truly lives up to its title of 'The English Riviera'.

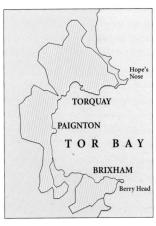

LEFT: Thatcher Rock, just south of Hope's Nose, is a familiar landmark in Tor Bay. The low profile of Berry Head can be seen in the distance.

FRONT COVER: Elegant terraces cluster on the seven hills surrounding Torquay harbour.

BACK COVER: A fishing boat sets out from Brixham harbour.

# TORQUAY

When Torre Abbey was founded in 1196, the Premonstratensian monks chose a gently sloping site, surrounded by steep, wooded hillsides and rocky valleys. Later, as the Abbey became increasingly prosperous, they built a small quay, not far from Tormohun, around which a tiny fishing hamlet became established. This marked the beginning of present-day Torquay.

There was little further development until the early 18th century, with the arrival of the Channel fleet. Neat new buildings, designed to accommodate the sailors and their visiting wives and sweethearts, began to appear on the hillsides. The number of visitors grew when the French ports were blockaded during the Napoleonic wars and those who were accustomed to travelling abroad discovered instead the delights of Torquay.

After the turnpiking of the roads in the mid-18th century, a new breed of visitor arrived – the wealthy invalid – drawn by the mild, soothing climate and invigorating sea air. This trend was boosted further by the opening of the railway in 1848 and Torquay, with its fine hotels, elegant terraces and Italianate villas, attracted an increasing number of gentlefolk intent on improving their health. Several of these original properties still stand among the tree-clad hills, notably Lisburne Crescent

and, the grandest of all, Hesketh Crescent, with its sweeping Regency façade.

At the beginning of this century, it was decided to cast off the Victorian image of this 'Queen of Watering Places'. Since then, with sympathetic development, Torquay has become a sophisticated modern resort while still retaining the charm and elegance of yesteryear.

The lively harbour, with its international marina, is the focus of activity and the Continental atmosphere is enhanced by the palm-lined promenade and the pavement cafés. The shopping facilities, many of which are under cover, are among the best in the West Country, restaurants, inns and wine bars abound and a variety of entertainment is available throughout the year.

Along the coast, there are no less than nine beaches, several in rocky coves or small bays, and all within easy reach of the centre, and fine clifftop walks offer spectacular views. Sailing is probably still the most popular pastime, but an increasing number of people are taking up sports such as water-skiing, wind-surfing and parascending.

RIGHT: The Pavilion, opened as a theatre in 1912, has lost none of its original splendour, although the Edwardian stalls have been replaced with an assortment of intriguing shops and the finely restored balcony area now houses a terraced café/restaurant.

FAR RIGHT: The pavement cafés by the harbourside enhance the continental atmosphere of Torquay.

INSET: The stylish open terraces of Fleet Walk, the newest under-cover shopping development in Torquay, complement the assortment of specialist shops, boutiques and cafés of its Winter Garden.

ABOVE: In medieval times, the picturesque village of Cockington, with its thatched cottages, ancient forge and stocks, was essentially an agricultural community, producing cider, wool and flour. The village became officially part of Torquay in 1928.

RIGHT: The remains of Torre Abbey date back to the late 12th century. Later additions include the gatehouse, the Mansion House, which now houses the borough's art collection, and the 'Spanish Barn', where Spanish prisoners-of-war were housed after the defeat of the Armada.

TOP RIGHT: Over thousands of years, the action of water on limestone has resulted in the astounding rock formations to be seen in Kent's Cavern. Remains of long-extinct mammals and a fragment of a human skull more than 12,000 years old were discovered here.

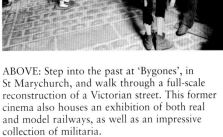

ABOVE: Step into the past at 'Bygones', in St Marychurch, and walk through a full-scale reconstruction of a Victorian street. This former cinema also houses an exhibition of both real and model railways, as well as an impressive collection of militaria.

LEFT: Babbacombe Model Village is a masterly portrayal of the English countryside in miniature. Thatched cottages, farms, a modern town – even Stonehenge – are sited in carefully landscaped gardens and a model railway passes over bridges, lakes and waterfalls.

ABOVE: Torre Abbey Sands, the main beach in Torquay, provides safe bathing for all ages and is ideal for wind-surfing and parascending. Harbreck Rock, a reef consisting of peat beds and a petrified forest, lies offshore and is accessible at low tide.

RIGHT: Nestling at the foot of Babbacombe Downs, Oddicombe Beach can be reached by foot along half a mile of zigzag road or by the Cliff Railway – a journey of a few minutes. The cliffs, of contrasting red sandstone and paler limestone, dominate the sandy shore.

TOP: Torquay has long been a haven for the yachtsman and the marina, built in 1987, will accommodate no less than 500 boats.

ABOVE: The Riviera Centre, which was built in the 1980s, offers a wide range of sporting facilities, including a leisure pool. There is also an exhibition area and a large auditorium.

LEFT: Redgate Beach, just south of Long Quarry Point, was a 'Ladies Bathing Place' in Victorian times. Gold has been found in small quantities in the rocks of the quarry but it is not economic to extract it.

Paignton Pier, overlooking Paignton Sands,
is a fine example of Victorian engineering.
It continues to draw a large number of visitors,
although its attractions nowadays are very
different from those originally offered.

Paignton, which lies in a relatively flat coastal plain, surrounded by low cliffs, was first settled by a Saxon, Paega, and was known as 'Paega's ton', or 'Paega's farmland'. By the time of the Norman Conquest it had been acquired by the Bishop of Exeter – in fact, he and his entourage were probably the first summer visitors! Its fertile soil and sunny, sheltered aspect proved ideal for growing grapes and other agricultural produce. Indeed, Paignton was once renowned for its cider and cabbages!

The small fishing harbour, built in 1838, once provided a base for seine-netting. Nowadays, apart from a small trade in shellfish, it is used mainly by pleasure-boats and ferries.

With the coming of the railway in 1859, Paignton began to develop into a large and fashionable resort. Marshland was reclaimed and the building of villas, hotels and grandiose residences proceeded apace. Nevertheless, the old area of Paignton's Well, around the Parish Church, has remained the heart of the town. Here can be seen the original Parish Prison, the remains of the old Bishop's Palace, and charming cottages, some dating from the 16th century.

Today, Paignton is a thriving seaside resort offering all the essential ingredients for an unforgettable family holiday. There are miles of clean, sandy beaches, from Paignton Sands and Preston Sands in the north to Broadsands and Elberry Cove in the south. Most are gently shelving and paddler-friendly, and boats and pedaloes are available for hire.

Apart from hotels and guest-houses, there are numerous self-catering holiday centres around the town and entertainment is provided throughout the summer for the benefit of visitors. Children can take part in the varied programme of events at Paignton Green, watch old-time Punch-and-Judy on the sands, or experience the many thrills and spills that await them at Quaywest Beach Resort. Spectacular firework displays are a popular feature during summer evenings and the Festival Theatre stages regular productions.

LEFT: Shipwreck Island, an open-air water-theme park with half a mile of breath-taking water slides, stands at the heart of Quaywest Beach Resort. Among the many other attractions are the Bumper Boats and Grand Prix Go-Karts.

LEFT INSET: Tidy rows of white beach huts with gaily painted doors line the promenade of Marine Parade and Preston Green.

In the warm glow of evening, with the boats
safely at their moorings, the lights of Torquay
and distant Torre Abbey Sands sparkle like
jewels across the water.

ABOVE: In the shelter of Roundham Head lies Paignton's small but busy harbour where fishermen sell freshly caught crabs and lobsters. Various pleasure boats operate from here and the wonders of undersea life can be seen in the nearby Aquarium.

RIGHT: Oldway Mansion, built in 1874 for Isaac Singer, of sewing-machine fame, owes much to French architectural styles. It now houses Council offices but many of the elegant rooms, as well as the beautiful gardens, are open to the public.

BELOW: The so-called 'Coverdale' Tower is nearly all that remains of the medieval palace of the Bishop of Exeter. Its association with Coverdale, who contributed to the translation of the Geneva Bible, is extremely dubious.

BOTTOM LEFT: The church of St John's, built of local red sandstone, was heavily restored in the 19th century. The west door is practically all that remains of the original Norman building.

BOTTOM RIGHT: Standing in the old quarters of Paignton, Kirkham House was probably built in the late 14th century. It was restored in 1960, refurnished in period style, and is now occasionally open to the public.

The smugglers of Paignton once landed their
contraband at Goodrington Sands. It is now a
paradise for children, with many entertainments
during the summer.

LEFT: Just beyond Paignton harbour is Fairy Cove – a delightful spot for children – with a gently shelving beach and plenty of rock pools to explore.

BELOW: The Cliff Gardens on Roundham Head, which lies between Paignton and Goodrington, support a fine collection of subtropical plants, shrubs and trees. These were originally donated by Herbert Whitley, founder of Paignton Zoo.

ABOVE: Paignton Zoo, which was opened in 1923, houses over 300 species of animals in its botanical gardens and a nature trail runs through 25 acres of native woodland. The new big-cat enclosure, opened in 1996, is part of a major refurbishment.

LEFT: The Paignton and Dartmouth Steam Railway offers the best of the old Great Western Railway. The 7-mile route to Dartmouth, along the spectacular Tor Bay coastline and the Dart Valley, is probably the most scenic in the country.

# BRIXHAM

Sheltered by rugged cliffs, the picturesque town of Brixham has a proud maritime history spanning some nine centuries. The original settlement, now known as Higher Brixham, grew up around a tidal creek from where the fishermen plied their trade, using lines and seine nets. Brixham fishermen were the pioneers of trawling, and the wooden-hulled Brixham trawlers, with their tan sails, were once the fastest, most efficient fishing vessels in the British Isles.

The tidal creek has long since been reclaimed for building and, although fishing is still a major activity, the town has found a new prosperity in welcoming visitors. Life in Brixham still revolves around the harbour but yachts and pleasure-craft now mingle with the fishing-boats and the quay is lined with cafés and pubs, amusement arcades and a pleasing variety of shops. Nearer the waterside, artists mingle with the shellfish- and ice-cream-vendors. On the surrounding hillsides there are narrow, terraced streets, linked by steep inclines or flights of steps, where shops and cafés, guest-houses and neat rows of fishermen's cottages jostle for attention.

A harbour walkway runs from beneath Furzeham, where iron ore was once mined, past the yacht club, to the Fishing Harbour. It continues around the Inner Harbour and its various attractions, past the South Devon Control Centre of HM Coastguard, Grenville House activities centre (once the Brixham Seamen's Boys' Home) and the Breakwater, to the foot of Berry Head.

Not far from here are two limestone caves – Ash Hole Cavern and Brixham Cavern – where the discovery of prehistoric animal remains shed new light on the antiquity of man. Signs of early settlement have also been found on the formidable grey limestone promontory of Berry Head, now a Country Park. Earthworks, together with finds of coins and pottery, point to the existence of an early Iron Age fortification that probably pre-dated the Roman invasion. Of further interest to the historian are the remains of two impressive Napoleonic forts, now subject to a preservation order. The park is also a National Nature Reserve, home to vast colonies of seabirds and many rare species of plants.

LEFT: One of the most important events in Tor Bay's history is the landing of William of Orange at Brixham in 1688, ostensibly to protect Protestantism and parliamentary liberties. The statue on Brixham quay was erected on the bicentenary of his landing.

RIGHT INSET: The *Golden Hind*, a full-sized replica of Sir Francis Drake's ship, was adapted from an old trawler. Below decks are displays featuring various aspects of sea-faring history.

Beneath the neat rows of houses on the hillside, the old harbour of Brixham is a constant hive of activity. While boats of all descriptions busy themselves on the water, visitors can enjoy the many delights of the quayside, such as the *Golden Hind*.

Below the Churston Golf Course lies Churston Cove, where the soldiers of William of Orange landed in the late 17th century.

ABOVE: More than a hundred diesel-powered fishing vessels are registered at Brixham and their activities can be viewed from an observation point on New Pier. To landward of the fishing harbour is the long-established Royal National Mission to Deep Sea Fishermen.

FAR LEFT: From the New Pier, regular ferries take passengers on the short journeys to Torquay and Paignton. There are also excursions along the magnificent South Devon coast to Dartmouth, as well as fishing expeditions in Tor Bay and the Channel.

CENTRE: The coastal path runs above Fishcombe Cove, one of the most charming in the whole of Tor Bay.

LEFT: Sheltered by the breakwater, the Prince William Marina can accommodate 550 boats and has full facilities for visiting yachtsmen, as well as an events pontoon for regattas, etc. The RNLI lifeboat is moored nearby.

RIGHT: The lighthouse on Berry Head is claimed to be the smallest (15 feet high), highest (about 200 feet above sea level) and lowest (the grandfather-clock-type mechanism is housed in a deep pit) in the West Country. The previous lighthouse, on the breakwater, was destroyed in a storm in 1866.

BELOW: The ruins of two Napoleonic forts stand on Berry Head. The guardhouse of the northernmost is now a café – possibly the safest and most secure in England!

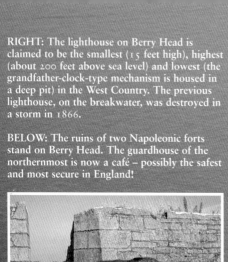